CAMBRIDGE LIBRARY COLLECTION

Books of enduring scholarly value

Spiritualism and Esoteric Knowledge

Magic, superstition, the occult sciences and esoteric knowledge appear regularly in the history of ideas alongside more established academic disciplines such as philosophy, natural history and theology. Particularly fascinating are periods of rapid scientific advances such as the Renaissance or the nineteenth century which also see a burgeoning of interest in the paranormal among the educated elite. This series provides primary texts and secondary sources for social historians and cultural anthropologists working in these areas, and all who wish for a wider understanding of the diverse intellectual and spiritual movements that formed a backdrop to the academic and political achievements of their day. It ranges from works on Babylonian and Jewish magic in the ancient world, through studies of sixteenth-century topics such as Cornelius Agrippa and the rapid spread of Rosicrucianism, to nineteenth-century publications by Sir Walter Scott and Sir Arthur Conan Doyle. Subjects include astrology, mesmerism, spiritualism, theosophy, clairvoyance, and ghost-seeing, as described both by their adherents and by sceptics.

Sleep and its Phenomena

James N. Pinkerton published *Sleep and its Phenomena* in 1839. The essay is a revision of a lecture first given to the medical faculty of the University of Edinburgh. In this work Pinkerton introduces his theory of types of sleep, analysing sleep in terms of its completeness. He follows with discussions of dreaming, sleepwalking, spectral illusions, sleep-time apparitions, hibernation and the sleep of plants, analysing each sleep-time activity in terms of sleep type. This work was one of the first to link the activities of the facial muscles and the nervous system during sleep with dreamed movements, thoughts and emotions. It was a pioneering work of nineteenth-century medical research into sleep and helped to establish Pinkerton's reputation. He is still well known today as one of the first to find a correspondence between sleep-actions and dreamed thoughts. It is an important work of Victorian medical research.

T0371367

Cambridge University Press has long been a pioneer in the reissuing of out-of-print titles from its own backlist, producing digital reprints of books that are still sought after by scholars and students but could not be reprinted economically using traditional technology. The Cambridge Library Collection extends this activity to a wider range of books which are still of importance to researchers and professionals, either for the source material they contain, or as landmarks in the history of their academic discipline.

Drawing from the world-renowned collections in the Cambridge University Library, and guided by the advice of experts in each subject area, Cambridge University Press is using state-of-the-art scanning machines in its own Printing House to capture the content of each book selected for inclusion. The files are processed to give a consistently clear, crisp image, and the books finished to the high quality standard for which the Press is recognised around the world. The latest print-on-demand technology ensures that the books will remain available indefinitely, and that orders for single or multiple copies can quickly be supplied.

The Cambridge Library Collection will bring back to life books of enduring scholarly value (including out-of-copyright works originally issued by other publishers) across a wide range of disciplines in the humanities and social sciences and in science and technology.

Sleep and its Phenomena

An Essay

J A M E S   N .   P I N K E R T O N

CAMBRIDGE
UNIVERSITY PRESS

CAMBRIDGE UNIVERSITY PRESS

Cambridge, New York, Melbourne, Madrid, Cape Town,
Singapore, São Paolo, Delhi, Tokyo, Mexico City

Published in the United States of America by Cambridge University Press, New York

www.cambridge.org
Information on this title: www.cambridge.org/9781108073103

© in this compilation Cambridge University Press 2011

This edition first published 1839
This digitally printed version 2011

ISBN 978-1-108-07310-3 Paperback

This book reproduces the text of the original edition. The content and language reflect
the beliefs, practices and terminology of their time, and have not been updated.

Cambridge University Press wishes to make clear that the book, unless originally published
by Cambridge, is not being republished by, in association or collaboration with, or
with the endorsement or approval of, the original publisher or its successors in title.

SLEEP AND ITS PHENOMENA.

An Essay.

———

BY

JAMES N. PINKERTON, M.D.

———

" ———Sleep hath its own world,
And a wide realm of wild reality."——BYRON.

London:

EDMUND FRY AND SON.

MDCCCXXXIX.

PREFACE.

The following Essay being one of those which met with the particular approbation of the Medical Faculty of Edinburgh, the Author has been induced to lay it before the public, after making considerable additions, and carefully revising it.

London, June 1839.

CONTENTS.

SLEEP AND ITS PHENOMENA.

CHAPTER I.

ON SLEEP.

" Le Sommeil, qui avec l'état opposé qu'on appelle
la vielle, se partage la vie de l'homme et des ani-
maux, est un des phenoménes les plus curieux de la
Physiologie."

ADELON.

THE Phenomena of Sleep present a most
interesting subject of inquiry; one, which is
alike within the limits of the Metaphysician,
the Physiologist, and the Physician.

Man not being capable of constantly exerting
his powers of sense and volition, a necessary
suspension of these functions occurs at intervals, which, for the time, deprives him of all
consciousness of his being, and during the con-

B

tinuance of which, the powers of the muscles and nervous system, previously exhausted by exercise, become restored. This state of suspension is denominated *sleep,* and is necessary to the existence of every animal as well as man. The approach of sleep is indicated by a peculiar feeling of languor and desire for rest. An incapacity for exercise of any kind, either mental or bodily, succeeds, the mind becomes unable to pursue any regular train of ideas, the limbs feel fatigued, and seek to dispose themselves in the most favourable position for inaction. A tendency to frequent yawning ensues, the muscles relax and no longer sustain or direct the parts to which they are attached; the head nods, the jaw is dropped, and the standing posture cannot longer be maintained; the eyelids close, and the senses gradually become unconscious of external impression, the sight first, then taste, smell, hearing, and touch in succession; the imagination rambles, and the ideas becoming confused, give rise to images of a most perplexing description. In this state they continue for some time, until, sleep becoming more profound, the images wax fainter and fainter, till they entirely disappear; the brain is left to thorough repose, and utter unconsciousness ensues. This is what is termed complete sleep. In incomplete sleep, or dreaming, some of the mental faculties continue in activity while the remainder are in repose, and the senses and the volition are either suspended or in action, according to the circumstances of the case.

Sleep being essential to existence, naturally takes place at stated periods, which may be, to a certain degree, extended by the will, or by circumstances hereafter to be mentioned. A celebrated author,* writes: "Animal existence is made up of action and slumber; nature has provided a season for each. An animal, which

* Dr. Paley.

stood not in need of rest, would always live in
day-light. An animal, which though made for
action, and delighting in action, must have its
strength repaired by sleep, meets by its constitution, the returns of day and night. In
the human species, for instance, were the bustle,
the labour, the motion of life upheld by the con-
stant presence of light, sleep could not be enjoyed without being disturbed by noise, and
without expense of that time which the eager-
ness of private interest would not contentedly
resign. It is happy, therefore, for this part of
the creation, I mean that it is conformable to
the frame and wants of their constitution, that
nature, by the very disposition of her elements,
has commanded, as it were, and imposed upon
them, at moderate intervals, a general intermission of their toils, their occupations and
pursuits." The approach of night is accompanied by a darkness, a cessation of activity
and universal silence, which allow of sleep being

enjoyed without interruption and without loss. Thus then night is the proper time for sleep; and accordingly at its approach all animated nature sinks into repose.

We are, however, acquainted with several causes which tend to produce sleep or hasten its approach, of which the following are the principal :—

Fatigue, (when not excessive,) either of the body or mind, promotes sleep.

Heat, especially when combined with a vitiated atmosphere, as in large and crowded assemblies, has a strong tendency to produce sleep.

Intense and Protracted Cold induces a dangerous sleep, not easily broken, and frequently terminating in death. Persons exposed to intense cold for any length of time, feel an overpowering sense of drowsiness stealing over them, which, if yielded to, inevitably terminates fatally.

Darkness, when combined with silence, or any regular monotonous sound, such as the murmuring of a river, the hum of insects, or the tolling of a distant bell, favours the approach of sleep: Whatever relaxes the body, such as warm bathing, fomentations, gratified desires, appeased appetite, a heavy meal, especially on a weak stomach, tends to the same purpose. There is also a class of medicines called narcotics, which by acting specifically on the nervous system, induce sleep. Such are opium, hyoscyamus, belladonna, aconite, conium maculatum, lettuce, hops, &c., also camphor, alcohol, and certain deleterious gases. Any determination of blood to the head, occasioned by whirling round, swinging, or the like, produces first giddiness, and subsequently sleep.

Some authors have defined apoplexy to be a state of profound sleep, induced by pressure on the brain; but it is to be observed, that the state produced by compression of the brain,

although resembling sleep in the partial extinc-
tion of the faculties, differs from it in many
essential circumstances. The one is a natural,
the other is a morbid state of the system; and
those cases in which stupor is produced by pressure on the brain, are regarded as indicating
some of the most dangerous diseases; whereas
the state of sleep, being a natural and necessary
process of the animal economy, cannot be
regarded as either the cause or effect of any
morbid action.

The system undergoes certain changes during
sleep. The circulation becomes retarded, the
pulse being slower and fuller than in the waking
state. The respiration is also slower, and, in
some individuals, more laborious and stronger,
as is shewn by their snoring. Absorption is
increased during sleep. The secretions are
diminished, with the exception of that of the
skin; for we find that the cutaneous vessels being
relaxed during this state, secrete more profusely

than during the waking state; but the urinary,
salivary, mucous, and other secretions, take place
less copiously. The heat of the body is reduced,
and the vascular action of the brain diminished,
as was shewn in the case related by Blumenbach, of a person whose skull had been tre-
panned, and whose brain was observed to sink
whenever he was asleep, and swell again with
blood the moment he awoke. He inferred from
this, that a diminished supply of blood to the
head was the proximate cause of sleep; but the
alteration of the circulation cannot be viewed as a
cause, but as a consequence, of sleep; for, if the
activity of the brain be diminished, which is the
case in sleep, its circulation will also necessarily
be diminished, as it is an established fact, that
the degree of activity of any part, and the degree of its circulation, are exactly correspondent.
The functions of digestion and assimilation are
apparently promoted by sleep, not by a greater
secretion of the gastric juice, which, in common

with the other secretions, is perhaps, even less
copiously formed than during the waking state;
but, by the repose, both of body and mind,
attendant on sleep, and so conducive to digestion, promoting this function in such a manner
as to more than compensate for the lessened
secretion of the gastric juice.

It is the opinion of Dr. Macnish that we
rarely pass the whole of any one night in a state
of perfect sleep. "My reason," says he, "for
such a supposition is, that we very seldom remain
during the whole of that period in the position
in which we fall asleep. This change of posture
must have been occasioned by some emotion,
however obscure, affecting the mind, and through
it, the organs of volition; whereas, in complete
sleep, we experience no emotion whatever."

The senses are not always in an equal state
of unconsciousness during ordinary sleep; taste
and smell remain so the longest, next touch and
hearing, and, lastly, sight. It is well known,

that persons may sleep profoundly during the
loudest noises, frequently, even without being in
the habit of so doing. Soldiers and seamen
have been known to have slept during the
alarms of a battle, and mechanics occasionally
slumber soundly during the incessant din of
hammers, forges, blast-furnaces, and the like;
and yet, persons who can thus continue sleeping
during the loudest noises, will often start up
instantly at the slightest touch of any part of
their bodies. The most important of the sensi-
tive functions which is suspended during sleep,
is that of volition. We find that the muscles of
voluntary motion lose their power, and it is upon
this circumstance that their complete relaxation
depends. But this suspension of the power of
the will over the voluntary muscles may be
sometimes incomplete, as is frequently the case
during incomplete sleep. Thus we find persons
who have acquired the habit of sleeping whilst
riding on horseback. A medical friend of mine

assured me, that he once rode four miles whilst fast asleep, on his way home, after protracted professional engagements. It is also a common occurrence amongst the postillions in some parts of the continent to jog on for miles sleeping. Other individuals, again, can slumber standing; and travellers, without having previously been somnambulists, have been known to have walked a considerable space of their road whilst asleep. Galen relates, that after having rejected all stories of this kind as being unfounded, he himself experienced a similar occurrence, which led him to put more faith in the like recitals afterwards. Whilst travelling one night on foot, he fell asleep on the road, and walked for the distance of about a stadium in this state, and was only awakened by stumbling against a stone.* I lately had for a travelling companion, in a diligence in Germany, a native of that country,

* De motu Musculorum, lib. ii. c. 4.

who, whilst smoking his pipe, fell fast asleep,
and yet retained his pipe within his teeth, and
continued smoking the whole time; indeed,
similar instances are not rare in that country.

Professor Stewart, in his "Elements of Moral
Philosophy," supposes that the will is not
actually suspended during sleep, but that it
loses its influence over those faculties which are
subject to it during our waking state; but the
considerations which he offers in proof of his
opinion, merely tend to shew that this suspension
is not complete (as we have above stated to be
the case occasionally in incomplete sleep), but do
not prove that volition is not suspended during
profound sleep. At the same time, however,
that the exercise of the external senses and of
voluntary motion is either altogether or partially
suspended, the body appears to retain its suscep-
tibility to the usual external stimuli, and thus we
are sensible during sleep of pain and uneasiness
of various kinds; and although not awakened

by them, we may afterwards recollect them.
"These impressions," says Dr. Macnish, "caught
by the senses, often give rise to the most extraordinary mental combinations, and form the
ground-work of the most elaborate dreams."

Sleep has been frequently compared to death,
by poets and authors of all ages.

> "Stulte, quid est somnus, gelidæ nisi mortis imago?"
>   OVID.

And again, Cicero,—

> "Jam verò videtis, nihil esse morti tam simile quàm
> somnum."

The resemblance between sleep and death,
however, it need hardly be said, is chiefly appa-
rent; death being a total cessation of vitality,
whilst sleep may be designated as a state in which
the vital motions are to a certain degree diminished, although none of them are so far affected

as to interfere with the due exercise of the functions to which they are subservient.*

All animals pass some portion of their time in sleep. "I have often observed," says Dr. Paley, "and never observed but to admire, the satisfaction with which the greatest part of the irrational world yield to this soft necessity, this grateful vicissitude. How comfortably the birds of the air, for example, address themselves to the repose of the evening : with what alertness they resume the activity of the day. Nor does it disturb our argument to confess that certain species of animals are in motion during the night, and at rest during the day. With respect even to these, it is still true that there is a change of condition in the animal, and an external change corresponding with it: there is still the relation, though inverted."

* Bostock.

Serpents sleep more than men or birds: fishes require little sleep. Amongst our domestic animals, the horse requires least sleep (from three to four hours), and some horses never lie down The sleep of birds is light and of short continuance.

The immediate cause of sleep is yet in great obscurity, and the theories regarding it, though numerous, are still very unsatisfactory. The investigation of this subject is one of great interest to the philosopher as well as to the physiologist; and although Professor Stewart has declared it to be beyond the reach of the human faculties, we may consider it to be as legitimate an object of inquiry as other functions of the nervous system, and hope, that from the rapid advances made in physiological science in the present day, ere long some important discoveries may be made to elucidate this interesting subject.

The theories of the ancients regarding the proximate cause of sleep are not worth dwelling on, and we may at once touch on those of more modern times. Boerhaave conceived sleep to be caused by a deficient quantity of the nervous fluid or animal spirits being carried to the brain, but that this deficiency might arise from the pressure of the blood upon the brain not permitting the spirits to be conveyed to it, as well as from a deficiency of the spirits themselves. Blumenbach, as we have before stated, regards sleep as being occasioned by a diminished or impeded flow of arterial blood to the brain; whilst Haller, Hartley, and many other eminent men, have conceived it to depend upon an accumulation of blood in the vessels of the head pressing upon the brain, and thus impeding its functions. Bichât agrees essentially with Cullen in his theory of Sleep. He assumes that, since all the animal functions have alternations of action and repose, this intermission, if long continued, and especially if extended to any number of these functions, constitutes sleep; and that sleep is more or less profound, according to the number of functions suspended. We will conclude this subject with some excellent remarks made by Dr. Bostock,* in reference to this opinion:—" We are led to regard the different functions of the animal economy as producing their ultimate effect by a kind of mutual action and re-action, one serving, as it were, to counterbalance another, so as to form an harmonious result from the combined operation of the whole. In this way, the sources of expenditure are adjusted to those of supply, and we shall always find that there is some method of providing for the regulation of any excess or defect that may take place. Many facts lead us to conclude it to be a general law of the nervous system, that it is incapable of acting for any length of time, without being exhausted, and requiring an alternation of re-

* Physiology. 3rd Edition, p. 816.

c

pose. This applies equally to the organs of sense, to the muscles that are under the control of the will, and to the intellectual powers. Now, during our waking hours, a variety of actions are going on, which tend to produce this exhaustion, and sleep is the period when the nervous functions are recruited."

CHAPTER II.

ON DREAMING.

" When Reason sleeps our mimic fancy wakes,
Supplies her part, and wild ideas takes
From words and things ill suited and misjoined,
The anarchy of thought, and chaos of the mind."

" And dreams in their development have breath,
And tears, and tortures, and the touch of joy."
BYRON.

DREAMS may be said to consist of a succession
of ideas passing through the mind with various
degrees of rapidity and vividness, and without
any regard to congruity ; and, uninterrupted,
as our waking thoughts are, by the voluntary
efforts which we make to alter the course of our
ideas, by comparing them together, dismissing
some, and calling up others at our pleasure.

c 2

The commencement of dreaming seems not unfrequently to depend upon some feeling excited in a part of the body, upon an impression made upon an organ of sense, or, upon indigestion, feverishness, or any internal irritation, but we cannot easily account for the direction which the ideas afterwards follow. Some persons are not conscious of having ever dreamed, others only when their health is disordered, whilst some again never sleep, for however short a period, without dreaming. It is supposed that children dream almost from their birth, and we know that sometimes dreams make such a powerful impression on their minds at a very early age, as to be vividly remembered in after years. Judging also from the motions and noises some animals, such as horses, dogs, &c. make during their sleep, we may infer, that they too have their dreams; however, on this subject there will always remain great room for speculation, as nothing can be positively known.

Impressions made on the senses, during sleep
are not unfrequently a cause of dreaming. Professor Stewart relates an instance of a friend of
his, who having occasion, in consequence of indis-
position, to apply a bottle of hot water to his
feet when he went to bed, dreamed that he was
making a journey to Mount Etna, and that
he found the heat of the ground almost in-
supportable; and of another person who having
a blister applied to his head, dreamed that he
was scalped by a party of Indians.

Intoxicating agents, heavy suppers, strange
beds, mental anxiety, or deprivation of customary stimuli, generally induce dreaming.
But very frequently dreams arise without any
assignable cause, and seem chiefly to consist
of old conceptions and associations following
one another, and appearing in various new
combinations, in a manner, over which we have
not the slightest control. During our waking state, our thoughts are in a great measure

confined to words; but, in dreaming, or even
in that state of partial delirium which precedes
it, the association of our ideas takes a flight,
more rapid, spiritual, and short; and in this
state we may imagine by a few hieroglyphic
unconnected pictures, more in a few moments
than we could express by words when awake
in as many hours. Thus we read of a case
of an individual, who once saw in a dream,
of a few minutes duration, all the events of his
previous life, brought before him in a succession
of vivid tableaux, most accurately and minutely,
even representing many circumstances which he
had entirely forgotten. He awoke from the
intense impression this dream made on him,
but after awhile he fell asleep again. He now
dreamed that he saw in a similar series of pictures, the history of all the persons living or
dead that he had ever known; and, awakening
anew in great anxiety, found he had only slept
a few minutes. Towards morning he fell asleep

a third time, and in another dream, not only
remembered his former visions, but composed
a poem on them, and set it to music, which
work he found, on awakening, he had com-
pleted in a few minutes, and the impression of
which remained so vividly, that he was able to
commit poem and music to paper without
difficulty.*

Dreams differ from our waking thoughts
principally in the following circumstances:
They are so much more vivid, that we mistake
that which is merely passing through our minds,
for an actual representation. Since also in sleep
the senses are not capable of receiving external
impressions, and although many of the mental
powers may retain their activity, the exercise of
volition is suspended, we find that in our dreams
we are perpetually falling into the grossest in-

* Moritz Magazin zur Erfahrung Seelen Kunde,
vol. v. p. 55.

consistencies, both in regard to time and place, and frequently imagine persons to be living, whom we know to be dead. In the same manner, from the suspension of volition, and consequently, from not being able to compare our ideas with each other, we frequently find our passions proceeding without our control, with an impetuosity quite disproportioned to the exciting cause. It has been observed also, that we pass through the most wonderful and improbable adventures in our dreams without feeling the slightest surprise, or being at all aware of their singularity or absurdity. In reference to this, Dr. Philip* remarks, "Why should we be surprised at our moving through the air, when we are not aware that we have not always done so? The mind of the dreamer differs from that of the infant in having been variously impressed, and therefore in the capa-

* Philip on Sleep and Death.

bility of having its impressions recalled. But
it is only as far as it is excited, that any impression can be recalled. With this exception,
it is as void of the results of experience as the
mind of the infant; and, therefore, in its partial
excitement, of the means of correcting any train
of ideas which that partial excitement suggests.
In general there is neither time nor subject for
reflection." Again, in the waking state, our
thoughts are in a great measure directed by
association, but at every moment, our senses
convey to us the impression of external objects,
and, by the agency of the will, we are perpetually directing the train of our ideas into
some channel, different from that into which
it would flow of its own accord. Were it not
indeed, that our ideas of perception are constantly correcting those of imagination, our
ordinary trains of thought, would combine to
constitute existence one continued dream, and
we should be no more sensible of the lapse of

time, or the due connection of events and circumstances, than we are when actually dreaming.
However vivid our ideas may be during waking,
we never mistake them for perceptions, and
thus we become sensible of the differences between them. Our notions of time and space,
during the waking state, are affected by events
passing around us, and depend upon the com-
parison we institute between these and our
internal feelings. Hence, we may explain the
absurd ideas we entertain regarding time and
space, in our dreams.

We not unfrequently find, that any sudden
sound occurring when we are asleep, may have
the effect of both awakening us and being the
cause of a dream, consisting of a train of actions,
which it would take sometimes even weeks
to accomplish. Dr. Abercrombie relates a
remarkable instance of this kind, " a gentleman
dreamed that he had enlisted as a soldier, joined
his regiment, deserted, was apprehended, carried

back, tried, condemned to be shot, and at last led out for execution. After all the usual preparations, a gun was fired, he awoke with the report, and found that a noise in the adjoining room, had both produced the dream and awaked him."*

The same author gives it as his opinion, that our dreams are chiefly occupied with objects of sight; " and I am not sure," he writes, " that we dream of tastes or smells, or even of sounds, unless when a sound actually takes place, as in several instances which have been mentioned. This indeed, only applies to simple sounds, for we certainly dream of persons speaking to us, and of understanding what they say,—but I am not sure that this is necessarily accompanied with a conception of sound." He then brings forward, in support of this opinion, an instance of an

* " Inquiries concerning the intellectual powers," p. 264.—3rd Edition.

acquaintance of his, a keen sportsman, who
frequently dreams of starting his game and
pointing his gun, but never succeeds in firing it,
it sometimes seems to miss fire, but in general
something appears to be wrong with the lock,
which renders it immovable. Experience,
however, goes to prove, that persons *may* dream
of sounds, even of the report of fire-arms, without any actual sounds existing at the time.
Thus I have myself dreamed of firing guns and
pistols with perfect success, when there was
no sound present to give rise to the dream. Not
long ago, for example, I dreamed I was about
to be attacked by an approaching party of
robbers, and snatching up a gun, I fired at them,
but unfortunately the gun missed fire, I tried
again, and again without success, and at last the
danger getting imminent, in desperation, I struck
the lock of the gun a violent blow with my fist,
when it went off, and I saw the foremost robber
drop down, and immediately after I awoke.

There are also many instances on record of
musicians, composing and playing their own
compositions in their dreams. Tartini, the
celebrated violin player, once dreamed that the
Devil appeared to him and challenged him to a
trial of skill. After playing his best, the
musician handed the violin to his satanic visitor,
who then played a piece with such skill, and of
such exquisite beauty, that Tartini awoke from
excess of delight. He immediately sat down
and noted down what he remembered of this
performance, which still goes by the name of the
" Devil's sonata." A somewhat similar instance
occurred to myself about ten months ago. I
dreamed that I was in a company, where our
conversation was about music, and whilst we
were discoursing, an officer, a stranger, entered
the room and joined us. After awhile he
observed, that since we all seemed so fond of
music, perhaps we might like to hear some; on
which he took up a lady's *worsted work frame,*

which was lying on the table, and held it to his chin in the manner of a violin, and then taking a common bit of stick he held it over the frame like a bow. After a moment's pause, and whilst we were watching his proceedings with astonishment, down came the stick on the edge of the frame, and then followed an air of such exquisite pathos and such divine tone, that I felt rivetted to the spot with delight. He went on to play a series of variations on this air with a brilliancy and execution, at the same time retaining the pathetic nature of the melody, in a manner that I had never before heard any approach to. At last my ecstacy rose to such a degree that I awoke at the sound of my own voice crying bravo! and found myself sitting up in the bed with my hands joined as if in applause. I felt so excited by this dream, that for several hours after, I could not fall asleep again, but lay thinking of the beauty of the melody I had heard, and humming over passages of it.

Towards morning, however, I fell asleep, but, when I arose, to my great disappointment I could not recollect the slightest snatch of the strange officer's air on the *worsted frame.*

Our dreams are generally more vivid and occur oftener towards morning, as sleep is then less profound, than during the early part of the night. A peculiar kind of dream occasionally occurs, during which the individual is impressed with the idea that it is only a dream, and if a disagreeable one, can sometimes by an effort awaken himself out of it. Thus, Dr. Beattie relates, that at one time he found himself in a dangerous situation upon the parapet of a bridge. Reflecting that he was not subject to pranks of this nature, he began to fancy that it might be a dream, and to dispel it, he determined to throw himself over, which he did, and it had the effect of awakening him. I have sometimes, in like manner, had a disagreeable dream, having at the same time the impression, that it was only a dream, and have forced myself to awake. But on several of these occasions, instead of actually awaking, I have, so to speak, awakened into another dream, and related to persons in this second dream, my former one. But in this second dream, the impression that I was dreaming never took place, and it was only on actually awakening, that I discovered I had had a *double dream.*

A belief in the prophetic power of dreams was universal amongst the ancients, and has been more or less continued to the present time, sometimes even amongst persons of education. Thus, we occasionally hear of individuals having had mysterious communications in their dreams, and events prophecied to them, which have actually come to pass. That such dreams have occurred, and do yet occur, we have no doubt, but we must regard the fulfilment of them as being entirely the result of accident; for, as Dr. Macnish observes—" any person who examines the nature of the human mind, and the manner in which it operates in dreams, must be convinced, that under no circumstances, except those of a miracle, in which the ordinary laws of nature are triumphed over, can such an event ever take place. The Sacred Writings testify that miracles were common in former times; but I believe, no man of sane mind will contend, that they ever occur in the present state of the world. In judging of these things as now constituted, we must discard supernatural influence altogether, and estimate events according to the general laws, which the Great Ruler of nature has appointed for the guidance of the universe. If, in the present day, it were possible to conceive a suspension of these laws, it must, as in former ages, be in reference to some great event, and to serve some mighty purpose connected with the general interests of the human race; but if faith is to be placed in modern miracles, we must suppose, that God suspended the above laws for the most trivial and useless of purposes; as, for instance, to intimate to a man that his grandmother will die on a particular day—that a favourite mare has broke her neck—that he has received a present of a brace of game—or that a certain friend will step in and take pot-luck with him on the morrow."*

Of the many thousands of dreams which nightly take place, it is not at all surprising, that occasionally *one* may become accidentally verified, which is then immediately cited as being supernatural; whilst those innumerable prophetic dreams which are not fulfilled, are never again heard of. The following is an excellent illustration of the fallacy of some of these prophetic dreams. It is to be found in a letter addressed to a friend of the writer, "On the Vanity of Dreams, and upon the Appearance of Spirits," published in " Le Mercure Gallante," for January, 1690.

* Macnish's Philosophy of Sleep, p. 133.—3rd Edition.

" The last proof, my dear friend," says the
writer, "which I can give on the vanity of
dreams, is my surviving after one that I experienced on the 22nd of September, 1679.   I
awoke on that day, at 5 o'clock in the morning,
and having fallen asleep again half an hour
after, I dreamt that I was in my bed, and that
the curtain of it was undrawn at the foot (two
circumstances which were true), and that I saw
one of my relations, who had died several years
before, enter the room, with a countenance as
sorrowful as it had formerly been joyous. She
seated herself at the foot of my bed, and looked
at me with pity. As I knew her to be dead, as
well in the dream as in reality, I judged by her
sorrow that she was going to announce some
bad news to me, and perhaps death; and fore-
seeing it with sufficient indifference,—' Ah,
well,' said I to her, 'I must die, then!' She
replied to me, 'It is true.' 'And when?'
retorted I; 'immediately?' 'To-day,' replied

she. I confess to you the time appeared short;
but without being concerned, I interrogated her
farther, and asked her, ' in what manner ?' She
murmured some words which I did not under-
stand, and at that moment I awoke. The
importance of a dream so precise, made me take
notice of my situation, and I remarked, that I
had lain down upon my right side, my body
extended, and both hands resting upon my
stomach. I rose to commit my dream to
writing, for fear of forgetting any part of it;
and finding it accompanied by all the circumstances which are attributed to mysterious and
divine missions, I was no sooner dressed than I
went to tell my sister-in-law, that, if serious
dreams were infallible warnings, she would have
no brother-in-law in twenty-four hours. I told
her afterwards all that had happened to me, and
likewise informed some of my friends, but without betraying the least alarm, and without
changing in any respect my usual conduct,—

resigning myself to the entire disposal of Providence." " Now," adds the writer, " if I had been weak enough to give up my mind to the idea that I was going to die, perhaps, *I should* have died."

There are, however, some very remarkable and well authenticated instances on record, of the accidental fulfilment of dreams, and we may cite as such, the following instances :

" Erasmus Francisci, when a youth, once dreamed that a person with a certain surname was about to shoot him, but was prevented by an aunt of Francisci, who snatched the gun out of his hands. Next morning the youth jokingly related this dream to his aunt, with whom he was living. She, however, saw it in a more serious light, and begged him to remain at home that day ; and as an inducement to do so, gave him the key of a closet in which she kept fruit. Francisci took the key and retired to his room, stopping, however, on his way, to speak with

his aunt's servant, who was cleaning two guns
in a room exactly opposite to his own. He
then entered his room, sat down to his desk, and
commenced reading. In a short while, however,
he remembered the key his aunt had given him,
and obeying a sudden impulse, he threw aside
the book, which was at other times a great
favourite, and proceeded to the closet. Scarcely
had he left his seat, when the gun which the
servant opposite was cleaning, and which, un-
known to him, was double loaded with bullets
for wolf-hunting, accidentally went off, and the
full charge passed through the wall and opposite room, in such a direction, that had Francisci
remained sitting, it would have passed through
his body. This servant happened also to bear
the same surname as the person in the dream." *

The following instance is related by Dr. Abercrombie :

* Schubert Symbolik des Traumes.

" A gentleman dreamed that the devil carried
him down to the bottom of a coal-pit, where he
threatened to burn him, unless he would agree
to give himself up to his service. This he refused
to do, and a *warm* altercation followed. He
was at last allowed to depart, upon condition of
sending down an individual, whom the devil
named, a worthless character well known in the
neighbourhood. A few days after, this person
was found drowned, and under circumstances
which gave every reason to believe that his death
had been voluntary."

The following is another very remarkable
instance:

" A lady fell asleep with a letter in her hand,
which she had that morning received from her
husband, who was at a distance. In this, she
was assured that he was in perfect health, nor
was there any likelihood of his incurring any
danger. Suddenly, she awoke, with a loud
cry, and on her female attendants running into

her room, they found her in a cold perspiration, bathed in tears. ' My husband is dead,' said she to them ; ' I saw him die—he was at a fountain, near which, grew several trees ; his face was deadly pale, and an officer in a blue dress was endeavouring to staunch the blood which was flowing from a large wound in his side ; he also gave him some water to drink out of his hat, and appeared to be deeply grieved on hearing him breathe his last sigh.' The attendants, and the lady's mother, who had by this time entered the room, in vain endeavoured to calm her apprehensions, by representing to her, that her dream was the consequence of her extreme solicitude for her husband, and that she had no cause for alarm, since but a few hours previously, she had received such good news from him. She re-mained, however, inconsolable, and continued to maintain that her husband was dead. Her mother remained by her bedside, and saw with pleasure, that after a copious flow of tears, she at last again fell asleep, quite exhausted with grief. Scarcely had she slept a quarter of an hour, when she was again awakened by the very same dream, and nothing could now persuade her that the vision was not supernatural. She was seized with a high fever, with continued delirium, and remained for fourteen days in a state bordering on death. In the meantime, accounts actually arrived that her husband had been killed on his journey.

" Four months of this lady's widowhood had passed away, when she one day went to hear mass in a neighbouring church. As the service was about to conclude, she got a glimpse of an officer taking a chair near her; on seeing whom, she uttered a loud cry and fainted. Her first words on her recovery, were to beg the surrounding persons to seek out the individual who had been the unintentional cause of her swooning, and entreat him to come to

her. The officer, who was still there, on
hearing that the lady wished to speak with
him, accompanied her to her residence. ' Oh !'
exclaimed the widow to her mother on reaching
the house, ' I have just now 'recognized the
person who received the last sigh of my poor
husband ;' and then turning round, at once
entreated him to give her the particulars of
that melancholy occurrence. The officer seemed
astonished at being recognized by a lady whom
he had never before seen, and begged to know
her name; on hearing which, he started. He
then related that accident brought him to the
place where her husband was lying wounded,
and he at once endeavoured to render him
every possible assistance. ' I saw him die,'
added he ; ' and although he was a stranger to
me, I could not but be affected when I found
that there was no hope of saving him. I left
him without discovering who he was; but
with his last sigh, he breathed your name,

which entered deeply into my memory, and which I recognized the instant you mentioned it.' This recital was frequently interrupted by the tears of the unhappy widow. The stranger was struck with the utmost astonishment, when she then most minutely related the particulars of her husband's death; and he immediately recollected the fountain, the trees, his own, and the dying man's relative positions, and even his own appearance at the time, which she described to him most accurately."*

It has not unfrequently occurred, that persons sleeping in the same room or house, or intimately connected, have, at the same time, dreamed similar dreams. An instance of this kind is given by Mr. Joseph Taylor. A young

* Moritz, Magazin, für Seelen Kunde, Vol. v. 2, 18.

man who was at an academy, a hundred miles
from home, dreamed that he went in the night
to his father's house, and finding the front
door closed, entered by the back door, and
went to his parents bedroom, and said, "mother,
I am going a long journey, and am come to
bid you good bye." On this, she answered,
under much agitation, "Oh, dear son, thou
art dead!" He then awoke, and thought no
more of his dream, until he received a letter
from his father, a few days after, inquiring
particularly after his health, as his mother,
on the same night on which his dream had
occurred, had dreamed that she heard some
one attempt to open the front door, then go
to the back door, and at last enter her bedroom. She then saw it was her son, who,
approaching her bedside, said, "mother, I am
going a long journey, and am come to bid
you good bye;" on which she exclaimed,

" Oh, dear son, thou art dead !" Nothing
unusual however, happened to the parties."*

There is a species of painful dream, to which
the name of incubus or nightmare has been
given. This is generally some hideous vision,
accompanied by difficult respiratory action,
sometimes even approaching to a sense of
suffocation; a great feeling of unaccountable
dread, and a sense of oppression and utter help-
lessness. In general, a person labouring under
an attack of nightmare, has the consciousness of
an inability to cry out; at other times, he fancies
he is shouting loudly, whereas, in reality, a few
smothered groans only escape him. As soon as
the faculty of exercising the voice, or voluntary
muscles returns, the paroxysm is at an end.
Nightmare, is accompanied by a feeling of

* Several interesting cases of persons having similar
dreams at the same time, occur in "Moritzs Magazin
für Seelen Kunde ;" See also " Schubert's Symbolik
des Traumes."

languor and inability to bring the voluntary muscles into action. It generally attacks persons when lying on their backs, especially after a full or indigestible meal; according to Dr. Macnish, however, it may also occur to persons sitting in a chair, or leaning their head forward on the table, and also when lying on the side. It seems to occur in postures in which the lungs are unusually compressed. It is also apt to occur in certain diseases, such as asthma, hydrothorax, and affections of the heart and lungs. Pregnant women are also liable to its attacks. Persons who keep late hours, study hard, eat heavy suppers, or are subject to any derangement of the stomach, or liver, are liable to attacks of nightmare. Sometimes this affection occurs in the day-time, in which case, however, the reason is always unclouded, whereas, in the night it is generally more or less disturbed. The following is a description of a daymare, by Dr. Macnish:—

" During the intensely hot summer of 1825,

I experienced an attack of daymare. Immediately after dining, I threw myself on my back upon a sofa, and, before I was aware, was seized with a difficult respiration, extreme dread, and utter incapability of motion or speech. I could neither move nor cry, while the breath came from my chest in broken and suffocating paroxysms. During all this time, I was perfectly awake; I saw the light glaring in at the windows in broad sultry streams; I felt the intense heat of the day pervading my frame; and heard distinctly the different noises in the street, and even the ticking of my own watch, which I had placed on the cushion beside me. I had, at the same time, the consciousness of flies buzzing around, and settling, with annoying pertinacity upon my face. During the whole fit, judgment was never for a moment suspended. I felt assured that I laboured under a species of incubus. I even endeavoured to reason myself out of the feeling of dread which filled my mind, and longed with insufferable ardour for some one to open the door, and dissolve the spell which bound me in its fetters. The fit did not continue above five minutes; by degrees I recovered the use of speech and motion, and as soon as they were so far restored as to enable me to call out and move my limbs, it wore insensibly away."* I have myself experienced several attacks of daymare, and in addition to the sensations described by Dr. Macnish, I had always a feeling of gradually sinking, as if dying. They generally came on when I was lying, or leaning in a chair, on my left side.

The proximate cause of nightmare is still obscure, and though many theories on this subject have been offered, they are as yet vague and unsatisfactory. It is probably occasioned by an impeded circulation of blood in the pulmonary arteries, by a distended stomach, compressing the diaphragm, by a torpor of the intercostal muscles, or perhaps by a combination

* Philosophy of Sleep, 159 page.— 3rd Edition.

of all these causes. Whatever may be the causes, however, their ultimate operation seems to be upon the lungs.

A state of mind somewhat analogous to that which prevails in dreaming, also takes place during what is called *Reverie*. In this, as in sleep, external objects make little or no impression upon the senses. Every person must have observed, that when alone, and while his attention is not called to any particular subject or object around him, and if he makes no voluntary exertion of mind to fix his attention upon one idea more than another, a rapid succession of different ideas, old and new, will take place in the course of a few minutes. Those also who have attended any public lecture, where the speaker has a dull monotonous delivery, must have been sensible of such involuntary successions of ideas taking place, when their attention has not been sufficiently fixed on what was spoken. Persons much addicted to severe study, and in the habit

E

of fixing their ideas constantly upon one subject
or another, when in a company where trifling
conversation is being carried on, will sometimes
find, that an involuntary current of ideas will
rapidly intrude upon their minds, and carry off
their attention entirely from what is passing
around them, and thus subject themselves to what
is commonly called *absence of mind.* In this
state, persons may suddenly burst out laughing
at an inappropriate period, or answer questions
put to them, from the subject passing in their
own minds at the time, and not at all in connection with the question put. Reverie differs
essentially, however, from dreaming in one particular, namely, that in the former, the faculty of
volition is in its full exercise, and it is owing to
this activity, that the insensibility to impressions
of external objects depends. Reverie sometimes
arises from peculiarity of temperament, and if
indulged in, soon becomes a habit not easily
broken off, and occasionally terminating in
actual imbecility.

CHAPTER III.

ON SOMNAMBULISM.

"Sunt enim qui dormientes resurgunt et ambulant, videntes eo modo quo qui vigilant."

———"I have seen her rise from her bed, throw her night gown upon her, unlock her closet, take forth paper, fold it, write upon it, read it, afterwards seal it, and again return to bed ; yet all this while in a most fast sleep.

MACBETH.

SOMNAMBULISM or sleep-walking is a peculiar kind of dreaming, to which some persons are liable. It appears to be an intermediate state between waking or sleep, in which the memory, the imagination, and the senses are in a sort of partial activity, and the will has a certain degree of power over the organs of voluntary motion, and even of speech, whilst the body seems to be more incapable of receiving external impressions than in ordinary sleep.

A variety of remarkable phenomena are presented in the different degrees of Somnambulism, which we will notice in the order in which they occur.

The first stage of somnambulism is sleep-talking; but this must not be confounded with the talking, which sometimes occurs in ordinary dreaming. Many persons laugh, or mutter a few sentences, or cry out, under the influence of a dream. The sleep-talking of a Somnambulist occurs during a profound sleep, from which it generally requires forcible means to arouse him, such as calling him loudly by name, shaking him, and the like; whereas, a person talking in his ordinary sleep, is in a state so nearly approaching to waking, as to be aroused by a slight touch or word, and frequently by the sound of his own voice, which is never the case with the Somnambulist.

Again, a person being awakened, whilst talking in his ordinary sleep, recovers almost

immediately the full possession of his faculties,
whereas, the Somnambulist, after being forcibly
aroused whilst speaking, remains for several
minutes stupified and confused. Another remarkable difference is to be found in the state
of the organ of hearing. Somnambulists, are
sometimes insensible to the loudest noises,
whereas, an ordinary dreamer sometimes hears
the slightest whisper which, not unfrequently,
is the origin of a dream. Dr. Abercrombie
mentions the case of a young officer in whom
any kind of dream could be produced by whis-
pering into his ear, especially if this were done
by a friend, with whose voice he was familiar.
These persons also, may sometimes answer
questions put to them in their sleep, but their
answers are unconnected and not to the purpose,
being given from their dream, whereas, somnambulists may be questioned loudly, and
answer in a rational connected manner, if the
questions refer to the subject they are engaged

with, or talking about.   There is a case recorded
of a servant girl, who, on sitting down, after
concluding her day's work, used to fall into a
deep sleep every evening ; and fancying herself in
her native country, held imaginary conversations
with her relations there.   If any person, with
whom she was well acquainted, entered into her
colloquies, she would discourse with them quite
rationally ; but this was not the case, if she was
accosted by any one with whom she was but
slightly acquainted.   These evening slumbers
rapidly became more profound, so that she could
hardly be aroused out of them, and would laugh
and shout, and be pulled about without awakening.   Her mistress alone could arouse her, by
calling her loudly by name.   When she awoke,
it was half an hour before she regained thorough
possession of her faculties.   This individual
afterwards became a complete somnambulist. *

* " Der Arzt." 74 p. 294.

There are many instances of persons having
delivered whole discourses whilst in this stage
of somnambulism. Dr. Haycock, of Oxford,
would give out a text in his sleep, and deliver a
good sermon upon it, nor could all the pinching
and pulling of his friends prevent him.*

Another similar case is recorded† of a basket
maker, who once heard a sermon which affected
him to tears :—the following night, he became
somnambulic, and repeated the whole sermon,
word for word, from beginning to end. His
wife in vain attempted to arouse him, and
interrupt his discourse. He continued, without
allowing himself to be disturbed, till the end
of it : but, after awhile, on awakening, he
was unconscious of having utterred a syllable.
From this time, he was seized with irresistible
fits of preaching, by day or night, at home or

* Macnish.

† Moritz Magazin, Vol. iii. Art. i. p. 44.

abroad, alone, or in company. These paroxysms occurred regularly, for many years,
three or four times a day, especially, if he had
been drinking any brandy. He was always
aware of their coming on and became anxious
in his demeanour, and withdrew, when he could,
as fast as possible from the society he happened
to be in. During these paroxysms, he was in
a state of complete insensibility to sound and
sight; and his eyes remained wide open and
fixed. At the conclusion of his discourses,
which generally lasted about a quarter of an
hour, he was very much exhausted. These
sermons usually consisted of reminiscences of
discourses, which he had heard forty years previously; and it was remarked, that his language
became more elevated and his pronunciation
better than when he was awake.

A writer, in " Fraser's Magazine," mentions
the case of an American lady, who preached

during her sleep, performing, regularly, every part of the Presbyterian service, from the psalm to the blessing.

In these cases, the memory seems to possess a remarkable power of recalling past events, and sentences, and conversations, to a degree quite unaccountable. These Somnambulists, also, sometimes express themselves with fluency on subjects, with which they had formerly shown but an imperfect acquaintance. An ignorant servant girl, mentioned by Dr. Dewar, during paroxysms of this kind, showed an astonishing knowledge of geography and astronomy, and expressed herself in her own language, in a manner, which though often ludicrous, shewed an understanding of the subject; for example, she explained the alternations of the seasons, by saying, that the earth was set *a-gee*. It was afterwards discovered, that her notions on these subjects, had been derived from over-hearing a tutor giving instructions to the young people of the family.*

It also sometimes happens that the musical powers of sleep-talkers are greatly increased. Thus, the servant girl, in the case first mentioned, could sing correctly during one of her paroxysms, any piece which she heard played over once or twice during the day, and with which she had no previous acquaintance. Dr. Abercrombie mentions a very remarkable and interesting case of a child, who during the night, uttered from her lips sounds similar to the violin ; and in this manner performed elaborate pieces of music, which she executed in a clear and accurate manner, and with a sound resembling the most delicate modulations of that instrument. She had some years previously slept in a chamber, separated by a thin partition from that of an itinerant fiddler of considerable skill,

* Abercrombie.

who used to spend part of the night in performing pieces of a refined description; but his performances were not taken notice of by the child at the time, except as a disagreeable noise.

The second stage of Somnambulism, is that from which it derives its name, viz.—sleep walking. In this stage, the individual rises from his bed, walks about the room, and performs various actions, generally those which he is in the habit of doing during the day. The freedom with which sleep-walkers perform muscular motions, is very remarkable, and they are frequently more adroit and active than when awake. We see them avoid every obstacle in their walks; open windows, walk along roofs, climb walls and precipices, and even swim, without awakening, and without evincing any fear at the perilous situations to which they sometimes attain.

Professor Fischer of Basel, relates that when he was a boy, at a seminary in Wurtemberg, a student from a superior college, came once on a visit to the school. This person who was strong and hardy, and appeared anything but nervous, was on his way home, whither he was sent to be cured of sleep-walking. He was in the habit of walking in his sleep, every evening at ten o'clock; half an hour previous to which, he used to experience an irresistible tendency to sleep, and was obliged to go to bed. Whilst on this visit, the boys of the seminary used to assemble at his bedside every evening at ten o'clock, to watch his proceedings, and exactly at that hour, he used to commence by uttering a few unconnected sentences, but he passed into the second stage of Somnambulism almost immediately and jumped out of bed. The scene of action was a large broad saloon, containing sixty beds, placed in four rows. He generally remained standing for a few seconds motionless, as if considering what to do, and would then suddenly make for the door or

window and endeavour to escape, or not unfrequently, if teased, commenced chasing the
boys. He would run up and down the saloon,
and between the rows of beds in all directions,
with amazing swiftness, followed by the sixty
boys, and then commenced a scene of shouting,
laughing, teazing and bolstering, during the
whole of which, the Somnambulist acted as if he
saw and heard everything, always avoiding
every obstacle with the greatest dexterity. The
Professor says, he remembers remarking that
he always went with his fingers spread out
before him. Sometimes the boys got him into a
corner and thought to secure him, but he always
eluded them by his superior dexterity in jumping
over the beds, or dodging between them. Occasionally, he contrived to escape at the door, in
which case, he generally ran along a passage to his
sitting room, where he rested himself, and not
unfrequently took down a book and commenced
reading, either in a low tone or aloud. His

eyes were alternately shut and open, but when the latter,they were convulsively turned upwards, shewing nothing but the whites, so that he could not have seen with them. One experiment which was tried upon this Somnambulist was followed by a remarkable effect. Imagining that it was by means of his finger points that he saw his way, the boys, one night during the sound sleep which preceded his sleep-walking, fastened a pair of gloves on his hands, and stockings on his feet. At the usual time, he jumped out of bed, but, in spite of their teazing him, he remained on the spot and commenced groping and feeling like a blind person. At last he seemed to discover what was the matter, and tore off the gloves in pieces, and threw them on the ground. The Professor does not remember whether he pulled the stockings off also,—however, immediately after freeing his hands, he commenced his usual wild career about the room.*

* "Fischer's Somnambulismus." 1839. page 74.

Sleep-walkers frequently endeavour to fulfil some of their customary daily occupations. An American farmer, mentioned by Professor Upham, rose in his sleep, went to his barn, and thrashed out in the dark, five bushels of rye, separating the grain from the straw, with the greatest correctness ; and Dr. Pritchard mentions a case of a man, who rose in his sleep, dressed himself, saddled his horse, and rode to a market place he was in the habit of attending once a week. Del Rio* relates a story of a schoolmaster, named Gundisalvus, who was in the habit of sleeping in a convent, and who so annoyed the monk, in whose cell he slept, by holding school out loud in his sleep, that the latter threatened to wake him with a rod. In the middle of the night, the monk fortunately awakening, beheld the school-master standing by the bedside, with a large

* Disq. Mag., Lib. i. cap. 3.

pair of scissars in his hand, and had just time to get behind the bed, when the schoolmaster struck the scissars several times with force into the pillow, and then returned to bed again. The next morning, for a long while he remembered nothing of what had passed, but at length, recollected that he had dreamed that the monk was come to beat him with the rod, and that he had defended himself with a pair of scissars.

A very dangerous inclination for climbing, is found in almost all sleep-walkers, whether on to the roof, or up precipices and rocks. This singular tendency has never been sufficiently accounted for. Sometimes, however, the climbing is occasioned in consequence of a dream; as in the case of a boy at Hamburgh, who once got out upon the roof, whilst asleep, at midnight, and laid himself down in the gutter for carrying the water off the roof, and remained there, without awakening, till noon

next day, in spite of a storm, which sent the
accumulated rain from two roofs over him.
He afterwards remembered to have dreamed,
that his master's canary had flown away, and
he had endeavoured to catch it.* The same
occurred in the case of a young nobleman, mentioned by Horstius, who was observed to rise in
his sleep and escape by the window to the roof,
where he destroyed a magpie's nest, brought
the young birds to his apartment, and then returned to bed. Next day he mentioned the
circumstance as having occurred in a dream,
and was only convinced that such was not the
case, by being shown the birds he brought with
him to his room. Sleep-climbers never evince
fear during their dangerous expeditions, but
frequently show great caution. A gardener,
mentioned by Dr. Knoll, was observed, whilst
climbing a roof in his sleep, to feel each tile, to

* Fischer's " Somnambulismus."

F

ascertain whether it was firm, and carefully to avoid those which appeared loose.

The third stage of somnambulism, is distinguished from the preceding, by its quieter course, and the greater degree of consistency observed in the actions of the individual. He now seems to be aware of his identity, so to speak, and acts in a manner similar to what he would during the day. He generally either repeats scenes from his day's occupation, or continues some work which he has begun. In the two former stages, his actions and ideas were those of a dream; but now, they assume the consistency of the waking state, and he seems to be quite aware of his name, station, and condition, and acts in accordance with them.

The following case of Negretti, a servant of the Marquis Sale, is related by Pegatti, in the July number of the " Journal Encyclopedique," 1762. When Negretti used to sit down in the evenings in the anti-room, he generally fell sound asleep. In about a quarter of an hour, he sat up, and remained a few moments, as if gazing intently at some object; he then got up and walked about the room, continuing fast asleep. On one occasion, he pulled out his snuff-box to take a pinch, but finding little in it, he went towards an empty chair, where a friend of his was in the habit of sitting, and mentioning his name, begged him for a pinch of snuff; a box was handed to him by one of the surrounding persons, and he took snuff. He then, all at once, assumed the attitude of a person listening; as soon as he had received his imaginary order, he took up a taper and went to a place where a light was usually kept. After he fancied he had lit his taper, he carried it through the saloon down stairs, stopping occasionally, and turning round, as if lighting somebody down the stair. On reaching the door, he stood aside, as if allowing the persons he had lighted, to go out; bowing to each, as in his imagination, they passed out. He then put out the taper, returned up stairs, and sat down. He repeated this scene twice that same evening. On another occasion, during one of these paroxysms, he made an excellent sallad, and sat down to eat. He had scarcely commenced, however, to do so, when the sallad was taken away from before him, and a dish of cabbage substituted; he did not notice the change at all, and in like manner, something else was set before him, in place of the cabbage, but he still fancied that he was eating sallad. During another paroxysm, he expressed himself unwell, and demanded wine; but drank water, without discovering the difference, and even expressed himself relieved by it.

The intellectual faculties appear to be sometimes even more developed in this state than during waking, and the memory remarkably vivid. Thus we find instances of Somnambulists having composed verses and solved mathematical problems, which they were unable to do when awake. Professor Wähner relates, that when a young man, he was once engaged for several days, in endeavouring to put a certain subject into two Greek verses, but without being able to accomplish the task. One morning, after having been fruitlessly employed in attempting it the night before, he went to his desk to make another effort, and found on it a piece of paper containing the two verses excellently composed, and in his own hand-writing. Quite astonished at this, he rung for his servant, who informed him that in the middle of the night he had rung the bell, demanded a light and sat down to his desk to write. This removed his doubts as to having written the verses, although he had not the slightest recollection of the occurrence.*

A gentleman at one of the English Universities had been very intent during the day in the

* Moritz Magazin. Vol. iii. Art. 1.

composition of some verses which he had not
been able to complete; during the following
night, he rose in his sleep and finished his composition; then expressed great exultation and
returned to bed.*   There is also a curious case
related by Heinrich ab Heer, of a Professor of
Poetry, who whenever he found any difficulty
in composition during the day, would rise at
night, dress himself and sit down to his desk,
and correct, improve, or continue the poem,
having done which, he would read it out loud
with great glee. After concluding, he would
restore everything to its right place, lock his
desk and return to bed.

Another excellent illustration is afforded in
the following case which is related in the
" Encyclopedie" under the article " Somnam-
bulisme." The Archbishop of Bourdeaux was at
college with a young student subject to walking
in his sleep. On planting himself from curiosity

* Abercrombie.

in the student's chamber, so as to ascertain his
motions, he observed the young man rise from
his bed and sit down to compose sermons, which
he read page by page, as he committed them to
paper, his eyes being at the same time perfectly
closed. On being dissatisfied with any passage
during the reading it over, he crossed it out and
wrote the correction very accurately above it.
The writer of this article saw the beginning of
one of these sermons in which was the following
amendment. It stood at first *ce divin enfant;*
on revisal, it struck the student to substitute
adorable for *divin,* so he crossed out the first
word, and wrote the second exactly above it.
But remarking that *ce* could not stand before
adorable, he very nicely added a *t* to *ce,* and
then it stood *cet adorable enfant.* To satisfy
himself that the Somnambulist in all these operations made no use of his eyes, the Archbishop
held something under his chin sufficient to
intercept his view of the paper he was writing
on; but he continued writing as before, uninter-

rupted by this obstacle in the way of his sight.
The Archbishop then took away the paper on
which he wrote, and substituted other papers.
Whenever these were of unequal size the Somnambulist appeared aware of the change, but
when they were equal, he wrote on, and made
corrections on the spots corresponding with his
own paper.—One night, having dreamed that he
was beside a river into which a child had fallen,he
went through all the actions tending to its rescue,
and with teeth chattering as from cold, demanded
a glass of brandy.   None being at hand, a glass
of water was given him instead ; but he immediately remarked the difference and with greater
impatience demanded brandy, saying, he should
die if none were given him.   Brandy was then
procured, which he took with pleasure, saying
as he smelled it, that he found himself already
better.   All this time he did not awake, but as
soon as the paroxysm was over, lay down in his
bed and slept very composedly.

The Somnambulist, in these cases, appears

to be alive to one kind of external impression ;
and the insensibility of the other parts of the
frame, seems to occasion a concentration, as it
were, of all the other senses into this one.
Hence, the accuracy and superior adroitness
with which those actions are performed, which
require the exercise of this particular sense, as
was the case of the student mentioned in the
last case, who, by a nicety of touch, or some
other perceptive power, discovered immediately,
without seeing them, the different sizes of the
papers that were put before him. It would
also seem, that in those cases, where the individuals composed better than when awake,
the total abstraction of the mind from surrounding objects, occasioned an unusual concentration
of ideas.

A higher degree of somnambulism, is that
which occurs in the day time. This comes
on sometimes suddenly, and is sometimes preceded by a sense of confusion in the head.

The following instance of this stage of somnambulism, is given by Dr. Müller, a Wurtemberg Physician.* A servant girl aged
fourteen, fell suddenly into a state of somnambulism, whilst in church. She had previously
been visiting the grave of her sister's child,
to which she had been much attached, and
by whose death she was deeply affected. She
rose from her seat during the service, and,
with her eyes closed, walked straight home
where she was found half undressed, lying on
the bed. She gave no answer on being spoken
to, and when raised up remained without
motion in the sitting posture. Thinking that
she was only in a profound sleep, the people
about her endeavoured to rouse her; but after
fruitless attempts to make her open her eyes,
they left her sitting, and watched her. In a
few minutes her head was suddenly drawn

* In Nasse's Archiv.

backwards by a spasm; and on this giving way, she jumped off the bed and endeavoured to escape, her eyes continuing firmly closed. On finding her intention frustrated, she quietly went to a table, and took up the hymn book which she had brought with her from church, and after turning over the leaves quickly, she found the place in which they had been singing, and commenced reading from where she had left off in church. She afterwards became liable to frequent paroxysms of somnambulism; on the 4th of April, 1824, she was sent by the clergyman, in whose service she was, to Dr. Müller, with a written statement of her affection. At the time she was sent, she happened to be in one of her paroxysms: she walked two miles and a half to the doctor's, and giving him the paper, remained without speaking. He read the statement, and wrote a prescription for her, which he told her to take to the apothecary's; but at the same time, he followed her himself,

to watch her proceedings. The girl delivered the
prescription at the apothecary's, and waiting for
the medicines, put them into her basket, and went
towards home, still continuing profoundly asleep.
The doctor followed her at the distance of about
fifteen or sixteen paces, and was astonished to ob-
serve, with what address she avoided the many
vehicles on the road, and got out of the way of all
obstacles, pursuing her road calmly and safely.
After walking for half an hour, she suddenly
awoke, and looked about her, bewildered and
alarmed. The doctor then went up to her and
accosted her, and found that she had no idea
how she had got there or where she had been to.
He then explained to her what had passed, and
giving her directions regarding the medicines,
sent her home, where she arrived awake.

Dr. Dyce of Aberdeen relates the case* of
a servant girl, who, during similar paroxysms

* Philosophical Transactions.

of day somnambulism, used to continue her usual occupations. At one time, she laid out the table for breakfast; and she repeatedly dressed herself and the children of the family, her eyes remaining firmly closed the whole time. It was, however, a remarkable feature in this girl's case, that, although during the intervals between these paroxysms, she had no recollection of what had occurred, yet during one of the paroxysms she had a distinct remembrance of what had occurred in the former ones. For instance, at one time she was taken to church whilst in this somnambulic state, and behaved there with propriety, evidently attending to the preacher, and during part of his discourse was affected by it to tears. In the succeeding interval, she had no recollection whatever of having been to church; but in the next paroxysm, she gave a most distinct account of the sermon, and mentioned particularly the part of it by which she had been so much affected.

Another very singular instance of day-somnambulism, occurs in the case of a rope-maker aged twenty-three years, which is recorded in the " Breslaw Acts."* This individual was liable, during two years and a half, to be affected in the following manner :—A profound sleep would suddenly come over him, whether at his work, standing, walking, or sitting, during which his senses received no external impressions, although he continued his usual occupation. On being seized by a paroxysm he knit his brows several times, and then his eyes closed; he next became entirely insensible to all pinching, pricking, violent shaking, and the like. A pistol fired close to his ear, or the most pungent aromatic held under his nostrils, produced no effect on him. If one of his paroxysms came on whilst he was at his work, he continued spinning and turning

* Acta Vratisl. 1725, Decembr. class iv. art. 7.

the threads as well as when awake, and if it
seized him whilst out walking, he continued,
slightly accelerating his pace, without deviating
from his right road, or stumbling against any
obstacle. He has frequently gone whilst asleep
from Naumburg to Weimar, and back again,
always avoiding the vehicles on the road with
perfect safety. On one occasion, his sleep came
over him whilst riding to Weimar; he continued his journey and rode through a small
wood, and across the river Ilme, stopping in
the middle of the stream to water his horse, and
lifting at the same time his legs to prevent their
getting wet. On his arrival at Weimar, still
asleep, he rode through several streets, and a
market place crowded with people, booths and
carts, but without sustaining the slightest injury;
and at last alighted at the house of a fellow
tradesman, where he had intended to go to.
He then tied his horse to the railing, and passed
through a crowded shop to the sitting room of

his friend. He remained here conversing for a few minutes, and then rose, saying he would return after going into the town to transact some business; which accordingly he did. On his return he awoke, and seemed surprised to find himself already there. On coming out of the paroxysm, his brow contracted as at the commencement of one, and he expressed himself much fatigued.

A very singular feature in this individual's case was, that sometimes, during one of his paroxysms, he would repeat and act all that he had said and done on some former occasion, most accurately. He did not confine these pantominic exhibitions to what had occurred during a waking interval, but used to repeat scenes of what he had done during some former paroxysm. Thus, on the evening of the day on which he had ridden the latter part of the journey to Weimar asleep, he went to visit a friend, who requested him to sit down, which he did.

After conversing about an hour, he suddenly
fell into one of his somnambulic paroxysms,
and then commencing from the time of getting
up in the morning, he repeated and re-acted all
he had said and done during the day. He
began by awakening his wife, rising, dressing
himself, repeating his devotions, and so on, till
he mounted his horse and bid his wife adieu.
Not a syllable of what he had uttered was forgotten, and he repeated his most trivial actions.
He continued re-acting his ride, his stopping in
the stream, &c., and repeated in like manner all
that happened after his falling asleep on the
road. All his transactions in Weimar, all
his visits were re-acted, till he came to the
house he was at the time visiting. He knocked
at the door, and spoke the same words he had
spoken on entering : he then took the same
chair he had taken on being asked to sit, and
repeated every syllable he had uttered whilst
sitting there, till the moment the paroxysm

came on, when he suddenly awoke, and had not the slightest knowledge of what he had done. During the whole of this singular exhibition his eyes had remained firmly closed, and he acted these scenes walking about the room. The only instance similar to the above, that I have met with, occurs in the case of a servant girl related by Dr. Abercrombie.*

" This woman was very much addicted to talking in her sleep ; and after some observation it was discovered, that, in doing so, she went over all the transactions of the preceding day ; everything, especially, that she had herself said, was distinctly repeated in the order in which she had spoken it. In general, she commenced immediately after she had fallen asleep, and began by repeating the first words she had spoken in the morning; and then went through

* On the Intellectual Powers. Third Edition, page 300.

the other conversation of the day, adapting her tone and manner to the real occurrences. Thus, whether she had called aloud to a person at a distance, or whispered something which she did not wish to be overheard — whether she had laughed or sung, everything was repeated in the order and in the tone of voice in which it had actually occurred. In repeating conversations with others, she regularly left intervals in her discourse, corresponding to the period when the other party was supposed to be replying; and she also left intervals between different conversations, shorter in reality, but corresponding in relative length to the intervals which had in fact taken place. Thus, if she had been for two hours without conversing with any other person, the interval in her nocturnal conversation was about ten minutes. In this manner she generally required about two hours to rehearse the occurrences of the day."

It is frequently a very dangerous thing to

arouse Somnambulists, and fatal accidents have sometimes been the consequence of so doing. When a sleep-walker is perceived in a dangerous situation, such as standing on a window ledge, or on the roof of a house, great care is to be taken in approaching him without giving him alarm, and he should, if possible, be gently led back to bed. Somnambulists occasionally possess preternatural strength during their paroxysms, and are enabled to wrench open doors, &c. which they could not effect when awake.

Considering the number of sleep-walkers, and their dangerous exploits, fewer accidents occur than might be expected; still, if they happen to awake whilst in some perilous situation, they generally lose their presence of mind from surprise or fright, and thus fatal accidents may take place. This happened a few years ago to a girl in Dresden, who was observed by her neighbours, to crawl along the roof of a house like a cat, for several successive nights, in perfect safety ; on one of these occasions, however, whilst getting in at the window of the garret, where she slept, she suddenly awoke, and immediately losing all presence of mind, she fell from a great height into the street, where she was completely dashed to pieces.

We are still in ignorance respecting the immediate cause of Somnambulism. It seems to be occasioned by some cerebral excitement, and, all causes which tend to produce this excitement, may be regarded as being capable of inducing Somnambulism. Sleep-walkers are generally pale, nervous, and irritable persons, more frequently women than men, and children above seven and adults, than younger children and the aged, who indeed may be said to be quite exempt from sleep-walking. Intense grief, sudden changes, violent passion, deep and tender affection, excess of intellectual labour, immoderate exercise, sensual excesses, abuse of spirituous liquors, too full meals, or indigestible suppers, all appear to favour Somnambulism. Sleep-walkers should, therefore, carefully avoid any of these causes, which may seem to have given rise to it. Most frequently, however, Somnambulism yields to no remedies, and wears itself out as the individual advances in age; or suddenly ceases without any obvious reason. All that can be done in these cases, is to guard the individuals as much as possible from accidents during the paroxysm.

A few remarks may here be made in regard to what has been termed *magnetic sleep;* a state, which, if it exist at all, is still in great obscurity, and affords ample room for impartial investigation.

It is said, that one person may, by the power of his will, accompanied by certain gestures, such as passing his hands down the course of the nerves of the members and trunk, or also by exercising pressure on certain parts of the body, induce in another person, first, an irresistible tendency to, followed by, profound sleep : if carried still further, different degrees of Somnambulism ensue. The person magnetizing, (as it has been termed), should be both mentally and physically stronger than the one operated upon, hence, women are generally the best subjects. . Magnetic sleep is said to be very profound, accompanied by convulsive motions of the body. The senses become so impenetrable, that in some instances, a pistol has been fired off close to the ear, and melted wax dropped on the body without producing any impression, although the individual hears the slightest word of the magnetizer.

Magnetic Somnambulism does not generally occur till the individual has been previously magnetized several times. In this stage, he is said to answer all questions put by the magnetizer, to foretell future events, to know other people's thoughts, to read books with his eyes

firmly closed, or with the book applied to the
epigastrium, to describe and prescribe for his
own internal diseases, without possessing any
previous knowledge of medicine, and even to see
objects at several miles distance. Various other
equally incredible powers have been ascribed to
persons under the influence of animal magnetism.
In reference to these phenomena, Rostan, in his
article on this subject, remarks : " Nous pensons
que *tous ces phenoménes appartiennent au
système nerveux*, dont toutes les fonctions ne
nous étaient point encore parfaitement connues ;
que *c'est à une modification, à une extension de
ce système et de ses propriétés qu'on doit
attribuer les effets dont nous parlons.*"

It is almost impossible for us, especially in
this country, where opportunities for observations on these phenomena are so limited, to
form any fixed idea on the subject of magnetic
sleep; and it must be allowed, that in the
numerous cases published on the continent, so

much has been proved to be the effects of the
imagination in weak minded persons, so much
exaggeration, and so much deception practised,
that, of the remaining quantity of actual fact,
there is still far from sufficient for us to form
any accurate or even plausible theory, and we
must at present content ourselves, till more light
be thrown on this curious subject, in not entirely
rejecting as nonsense what so many eminent
men on the continent, and latterly one or two
in this country, have received as actual physiological phenomena.

CHAPTER IV.

ON SPECTRAL ILLUSIONS.

"I have heard (but not believed) the spirits of the dead
May walk again :"—
WINTER'S TALE.

"Res mirandas imaginantur ; et putant se videre quae
nec vident, nec audiunt."
LAVATER " DE SPECTRIS."

WE find great controversies among authors
of all ages, concerning the existence or non-
existence, the possibility or non-possibility of
apparitions. The Chaldeans, Jews, and mostly
all eastern nations, have been staunch upholders
of the belief, that the spirits of the dead may
sometimes visit the living. Indeed, this belief
appears to have been supported in all ages, even
among the learned, to the present day.

Almost all the numerous cases of apparitions

recorded by authors, may be traced either to some false impression made upon the senses, to a sort of partial dreaming, or to other causes hereafter to be mentioned.

During partial darkness or obscurity, the sense of sight is very liable to be deceived, hence, dusk is the usual season in which apparitions are said to have appeared. Indeed, the state of the mind at that time is in a sort of way prepared for the admission of such delusions, and the imagination then frequently transforms inanimate objects into the semblance of the human figure: this, occurring to persons of a very nervous or imaginative disposition, would give them the impression of a living being, which by a sudden association, would seem to resemble some person, living or dead, in whom they are much interested.

" A gentleman, a friend of Dr. Andrew Combe, has in his house a number of phrenological casts, among which is particularly conspicuous, a bust of Curran. A servant girl, belonging to the family, after undergoing great fatigue, awoke early one morning, and beheld at the foot of her bed the apparition of Curran. He had the same pale and cadaverous aspect as in the bust, but he was now dressed in a sailor's jacket, and his face decorated with an immense pair of whiskers. In a state of extreme terror she awoke her fellow-servant, and asked if she did not see the spectre. She, however, saw nothing, and endeavoured to rally her out of her alarm ;—but the other persisted in the reality of the apparition, which continued visible for several minutes. The gentleman, it appears, at that time kept a pleasure yacht, the seamen belonging to which were frequently in the house. This, perhaps, was the origin of the sailor's dress in which the spectre appeared ;— and the immense whiskers had also probably been borrowed from one of these occasional visitors."*

* " Abercrombie."

Another instance, referable to the same cause is related by Dr. Ferriar.

A gentleman travelling in the Highlands of Scotland was conducted to a bedroom which was reported to be haunted by the spirit of a man who had there committed suicide. In the night he awoke under the influence of a frightful dream, and found himself sitting up in bed, with a pistol grasped in his right hand. On looking round the room, he now discovered by the moonlight, a corpse dressed in a shroud reared against the wall, close by the window ; the features of the body, and every part of the funeral apparel being perceived distinctly. On recovering from the first impulse of terror, so far as to investigate the source of the phantom, it was found to be produced by the moonbeams forming a long bright image through the broken window.

Next to the eye, the ear seems to be the most liable to false impressions, of the organs of sense. Dr. Johnson, while entering his chamber at

Oxford, once heard his mother who was then at
Litchfield, distinctly calling, Sam! and Dr.
Abercrombie mentions the case of a clergyman,
accustomed to full living, who was suddenly
seized with vomiting, vertigo, and ringing in
his ears, and continued in rather an alarming
condition for several days. During this time,
he had the sound in his ears of tunes most
distinctly played, and in accurate succession.

The sense of touch also, though seldomer, is
occasionally liable to perversion, so as to convey to the individual the idea of a supernatural
visitor. Thus, Sir Walter Scott relates the story
of a nobleman, who had fallen asleep with some
uneasy feelings arising from indigestion, which
operated in their usual course of visionary
terrors. At length, they were all summed up in
the apprehension, that the phantom of a dead
man held the sleeper by his wrist, and endeavoured to drag him out of bed. He awaked in
horror, and still felt the cold dead grasp of a

corpse's hand on his right wrist. It was a minute before he discovered that his own left hand was in a state of numbness, and with it he had accidentally encircled his right arm.*

Spectral illusions, however, are not always occasioned by the mere force of imagination, but there is a peculiar state in which the brain is morbidly affected, so as to convey false perceptions to the mind, but in which the mind is at the same time sound, and the individual is consequently aware of the fallacy of these perceptions. These generally consist of spectres, grotesque figures, or apparitions of deceased friends or relatives, and are sometimes accompanied by false perceptions of sound.

Many well authenticated instances of this kind occur, such as the well known case of Nicolai the Prussian Bookseller.†

* " Dæmonology and Witchcraft." 2nd edition. p. 44.
† " Nicholson's Journal." v. vi. page 161 et seq. et
v. xv. page 238 et seq.

Spectral illusions are also not unfrequently the concomitants of fevers and inflammatory attacks. An excellent example of this is related by Dr. Macnish of himself.

" In March, 1829, during an attack of fever, accompanied with violent action in the brain, I experienced illusions of a very peculiar kind. They did not appear except when the eyes were shut or the room perfectly dark; and this was one of the most distressing things connected with my illness; for it obliged me either to keep my eyes open or to admit more light into the chamber than they could well tolerate. I had the consciousness of shining and hideous faces grinning at me in the midst of profound darkness, from which they glared forth in horrid and diabolical relief. They were never stationary, but kept moving in the gloomy back ground; sometimes they approached within an inch or two of my face; at other times they receded several feet or yards

from it. They would frequently break into frag-
ments, which after floating about would unite—
portions of one face coalescing with those of
another, and thus forming still more uncouth
and abominable images. The only way I could
get rid of those phantoms, was by admitting more
light into the chamber and opening the eyes,
when they instantly vanished; but only to re-
appear when the room was darkened or the eyes
closed. One night, when the fever was at its
height, I had a splendid vision of a theatre, in
the arena of which Ducrow, the celebrated
equestrian, was performing. On this occasion I
had no consciousness of a dark back-ground like
to that on which the monstrous images floated,
but everything was gay, bright, and beautiful.
I was broad awake, my eyes were closed, and
yet I saw with perfect distinctness, the whole
scene going on in the theatre—Ducrow performing his wonders of horsemanship—and the
assembled multitude, among whom I recognized

H

several intimate friends; in short, the whole process of the entertainment as clearly as if I were present at it. When I opened my eyes, the whole scene vanished, like the enchanted palace of the Necromancer; but when I closed them it as distinctly returned. But though I could thus dissipate the spectacle, I found it impossible to get rid of the accompanying music. This was the grand march in the Opera of Aladdin, and was performed by the orchestra with more superb and imposing effect, and with greater loudness, than I ever heard it before; it was executed, indeed, with tremendous energy. This air I tried every effort to dissipate, by forcibly endeavouring to call other tunes to mind, but it was in vain. However completely the vision might be dispelled, the music remained in spite of every effort to banish it. During the whole of this singular state, I was perfectly aware of the illusiveness of my feelings, and though labouring under violent head-ache, could

not help speculating upon them, and endeavouring to trace them to their proper cause. This
theatrical vision continued for about five hours;
the previous delusions for a couple of days."*

A remarkable feature in the above case was
the strong illusion of hearing. Dr. Bostock†
relates, that at one time, whilst labouring under
a fever, attended with great debility of the
nervous system, and with a severe pain in the
head, after having passed a sleepless night, he
perceived figures presenting themselves before
him, similar to those described by Nicolai.
Being at the time free from delirium, and as
they continued visible for about three days and
nights with little intermission, he was able to
make observations regarding them. There were
two circumstances which appeared to him remarkable; first, that the spectral appearances

* "Philosophy of Sleep." p. 274. 3rd edition.
† Elements of Physiology   Third Edition, page 751.

always followed the motion of the eyes; and, secondly, that the objects which were the best defined, and remained the longest visible, were such as he had no recollection of having ever previously seen. For about twenty-four hours, he had constantly before him a human figure, the features and dress of which were as distinctly visible as that of any real existence, and of which, after an interval of many years, he still retained a most lively impression, although he had never discovered any person, whom he had previously seen, that resembled it. During one part of this disease, after the disappearance of this stationary phantom, a number of objects, principally human faces or figures, on a small scale, presented themselves before him like a succession of medallions. They were all of the same size, and appeared to be all situated at the same distance from the face. After one had been seen for a few minutes, it became fainter, and then another, which was more vivid, seemed to be laid upon it, or substituted in its place, which in its turn, was superseded by a new appearance. During all this succession of scenery, he did not see any object, as far as he could recollect, with which he had been previously acquainted, nor did those objects, with which his mind at other times was most occupied, present themselves. They appeared to be invariably new creations, or at least new combinations, of which he could not trace the original materials.

Dr. Abercrombie quotes the case of a lady mentioned in the Edinburgh Journal of Science, for April 1830, who had been for some time in bad health, being affected with pectoral complaints, and much nervous debility. This lady repeatedly heard her husband's voice calling her by name, as if from an adjoining room; and on one occasion, she saw his figure most distinctly standing before the fire in the drawing-room, when he had left the house half an hour before. She went

and sat down within two feet of the figure, and
was greatly astonished that he did not answer
when she spoke to him. The figure continued
visible for several minutes, then moved towards
a window at the farther end of the room, and
there disappeared. A few days after this appearance, she saw the figure of a cat lying on
the hearth-rug ; and, on another occasion, while
adjusting her hair before a mirror, late at night,
she saw the countenance of a friend, dressed in
a shroud, reflected from the mirror, as if looking
over her shoulder.

Perhaps one of the most startling of these
morbid impressions is the apparition of *one-
self*. This has not unfrequently happened, and
popular superstition considers this appearance a
sure foreboder of death.

Professor Fischer of Basel relates the case of
a lady of a melancholic temperament, who, from
living in the bustle of a town, was suddenly
removed, in consequence of marrying a country

clergyman, to a small solitary village in France, were she led a dull and miserable life. After having resided here for several weeks, the following occurrence happened to her. She went to the kitchen to bring up a dish whilst her husband and a guest were at dinner, and on approaching the dining-room, she beheld an apparition of *herself* on the opposite staircase, in exactly the same attitude, and with the same dish in its hand. She received such a fright from this startling appearance, that she immediately let fall the dish she was carrying and fainted away. On another occasion, she went up stairs to fetch a particular dress, in which she was going out driving, and on reaching her chamber, again saw herself, standing before the clothes closet, and in the identical dress she was going for. At first these apparitions were followed on each occasion by a severe illness; but at last, as they became more frequent, she grew quite indifferent to them, and on seeing this

double of herself, would merely exclaim, " Ha !
are you there again ?" Her medical attendant
advised her to remove from the place, and engage
in lively pursuits, which she did. In a year's
time she returned quite cured, and lived in the
same house for a quarter of a year, before re-
moving to a new one, without any repetition of
her former illusions.

In the affection called *delirium tremens,*
which is produced by a continued use, or
rather abuse, of intoxicating liquors, spectral
illusions are not at all unfrequent. The patient
frequently imagines that he sees rats, mice,
and all sorts of vermin running across the
bed clothes; or, that persons are lying in
wait to murder him, or sees hideous figures
grinning at him. In a case, however, described
by Dr. Combe, the illusive appearances were
of a more pleasing kind than generally happen.
The patient, an innkeeper, refused, during an
attack of delirium tremens, to allow Dr. Combe

to look at a blister, which had been placed
between his shoulders, " because he could not
take off his coat *before the ladies who were in
the room.*" When assured that there was no-
body there, he smiled at the joke, as he
conceived it to be, and on being questioned
about them, described them as several in
number, well dressed and good-looking. At
the Doctor's request he rose up to shake
hands with them, and was astonished at finding them elude his grasp, and his hand to
strike the wall. This, however, convinced him
that it was an illusion, and he forthwith took off
his coat, but was unwilling to converse longer
on the subject. In a few days the ladies
vanished from his sight.* I knew a case of a
blacksmith in Edinburgh, who, in a fit of delirium tremens, imagined himself to be a horse,
and jumping out of bed, escaped into a neigh-

* Macnish's " Philosophy of Sleep."

bouring green, and commenced neighing and
running about. After a smart chase he was
secured by some of the neighbours and brought
back to bed.

There are several poisons, particularly of the
narcotic kind, which when introduced into the
system by the organs of digestion, have the
effect of inducing delirium, and occasionally
spectral illusions.—The effect of opium is well
known in giving an impression of reality to the
visions of the imagination. Conium maculatum,
Hyoscyamus, Belladonna, and some others, have
been known to have the same effect. Dr.
Alderston of Hull was informed by a conjuror
of note, that he could give him a recipe for a
preparation of antimony, sulphur, &c., which,
when burnt in a confined room, would so affect
a person shut up in it, that he would fancy he
saw spectres and apparitions.

Spectral illusions sometimes occur also in
diseases of an apoplectic or epileptic character.

Dr. Gregory used to mention in his lectures, a gentleman liable to epileptic fits, in whom the paroxysm was generally preceded by the appearance of an old woman, who seemed to come up to him, and strike him on the head with her crutch ; and at that instant he fell down in the fit.*

Hypochondriacs and persons of a gloomy tendency of mind are apt to see and hear imaginary sights and sounds. Burton in his " Anatomy of Melancholy," gives the following description of such individuals :—" Those men are usually sad and solitary, and that continually, and in excess, more than ordinary suspicious, more fearful, and have long, sore, and most corrupt imaginations ; cold and black, bashful, and so solitary, that they will endure no company ; they dream of graves still, and dead men, and think themselves bewitched or dead ; if it be extream,

* Abercrombie.

they think they hear hideous noyses, see and talk with black men, and converse familiarly with devils; and such strange chimeras and visions, or that they are possessed by them, that some body talks to them or within them." *

In all cases of spectral illusions, occurring in diseases or from a bad state of health, they will be found to disappear with the removal of the malady.

* Burton's " Anatomy of Melancholy." 16th edition. page 265.

CHAPTER V.

ON HYBERNATION; AND THE SLEEP OF PLANTS.

" The power of cold in occasioning slumber, is not
confined to Man, but pervades a very extensive class
of animals."

MACNISH.

THERE is a singular state of the system, to
which certain animals are incident during the
cold season, in which the greater part of their
functions is apparently suspended, constituting
what has been termed *torpidity* or *hybernation*.
This does not appear to be confined to any
peculiarity of structure, or to any particular class
of animals, but seems rather to exist in cases
where the circumstances or situation of the
animal render it necessary for it to remain a
certain part of the year in a state of torpidity.

Hybernation has been generally supposed to bear a close analogy to sleep, and, though perhaps this idea may have been carried too far, yet to a certain extent, it appears to exist. It is a wise and benevolent provision for the preservation of certain animals, and must not be confounded with that sleep which precedes the death of persons who perish from cold : in the latter case, the vitality of the body is destroyed, and the sensations preceding insensibility are painful in the extreme; but far from being a painful state, hybernation is indeed a provision against suffering.

All the powers and functions of the animal are more or less affected during torpidity, and this appears to be the case with the respiration earliest. In proportion as the animal becomes torpid, the action of the lungs diminishes until it very nearly, or, according to Flourens and other authors, entirely ceases. The circulation, as well as the functions of digestion, secretion, and absorption are in like manner nearly suspended; the visible excretions are arrested and the temperature reduced nearly to the surrounding medium. The state of torpidity in all hybernating animals is preceded by a remarkable increase of fat, which seems to be laid up as a sort of protection for the vital organs against intense cold.

M. Mangili, an Italian naturalist, made some curious experiments upon the dormouse, and other hybernating animals. He kept a dormouse in a cupboard in his study. On the twenty-fourth of December, the thermometer being about 40° the dormouse curled itself up amongst a heap of papers and went to sleep. On the twenty-seventh, the thermometer being several degrees lower, M. Mangili ascertained that the animal breathed, and suspended its respiration at regular intervals;—that is, that after four minutes of perfect repose, in which it appeared as if dead, it breathed about twenty-four times in the space of a minute and a half, and then again its breathing was completely suspended, and again renewed. As the weather became milder, the intervals were reduced to three minutes; but when the thermometer fell nearly to the freezing point, the intervals were then six minutes. Within ten days from its beginning to sleep, (the weather then being very cold) the dormouse woke up and ate a little. It then went to sleep again, and occasionally wakened again through the winter. But as the season advanced, the intervals of perfect repose when no breathing could be perceived, were much longer, sometimes more than twenty minutes.

The Marmot, an inhabitant of some mountainous parts of Europe, makes no provision for the winter as the dormouse, but sleeps completely and continuously throughout the season.

The Bat affords a familiar instance of hybernation. On the approach of the cold evenings, at
the latter end of autumn, the torpidity of these
animals commences, and they are found clustered
together to defend themselves against the cold.
On the whole, they appear to fare better during
a severe winter, than a mild one; for, warm
weather not only awakens them, but re-excites
their digestive powers, at a time when the requisite supply of food is not attainable. Some
have been observed to come forth at the temperature of 42° Fahrenheit, and others only at
that of 48°. Such of them as have been roused
by irritation or sudden application of heat, have
seldom survived the third day, but then the
weather became colder again. They appear to
shrink during their torpidity from the touch, or
the approach of a lighted candle. Their posture
during this period is that of suspending
themselves by the hind claws, with the head
downwards.

The polar and brown bear, the hedgehog, the badger and the squirrel, are likewise hybernating animals; as also, the frog, the land tortoise, and almost all the individuals of the lizard, insect, and serpent tribes.

Want of moisture produces torpor in some animals ; such is the case with the garden snail, which indeed has been said to have been revived by being moistened with water, after having been dried for fifteen years. According to Spallanzani, animalculi have been recovered by moisture, after a torpor of twenty-seven years. Humboldt says, that the torpidity of the Boaconstrictor and Alligator during the dry season, is also produced by the lack of moisture. With birds, torpidity seldom occurs, probably, from the temperature of their blood being higher than that of other animals.

Various opinions have been formed respecting the cause of hybernation, for, although there seems to be a necessary connection between the reduced temperature and the torpidity of the functions ;—yet, we are unable to explain why certain animals only experience this effect, or what it is that enables them to retain their vital powers during this state, or how their bodies bear this suspension of the functions, without being decomposed, or their powers irrecoverably destroyed.

A period of rest seems to be as necessary to the vegetable kingdom as sleep is to animals. The rapid growth observable in plants during the night is a proof that the organs of assimilation had been partially interrupted in discharging their functions during the day when exposed to the action of heat and light, and other stimulants. During the night many plants are observed to change their appearances very considerably. Their leaves, according to the nature of the plant, droop, rise up, or fold themselves in various ways, for the protection of the flowers, the buds, the fruits, and young stems; and many flowers, to escape a super-abundance of moisture, hang down their mouths towards the earth, or wrap themselves up in their *calyces*. Instances of this kind of rest are constantly before our eyes. The trefoil, the oxalis, and other herbs with ternate leaves, sleep with their leaflets folded together in the erect posture; the lupin and convolvulus minor are also familiar instances. The leaves of plants assume different positions during the night, the object in general appearing to be the protection of some more delicate part of their structure from the effects of the night air. The tamarind closes its leaves over the fruit, the acacia does the same, while the intention in some others is the guarding the underside of the leaves from injury. A singular instance of this state of plants, and which first attracted the notice of the great Linnæus, occurred in a species of water lily, *lotus ornithopodioides*. The plant being rare was much prized by its owner, and two blossoms appearing on it, the gardener was particularly cautioned to take care and prevent any accident occurring to it, until more notice could be taken of it. Business prevented its being thought of until evening, but when it was produced, no blossom was visible. The next day the flowers were again seen, but in the evening were not to be found; the third day the same thing occurred; but after a very minute search, each blossom was found hidden under three leaves, as if covered with a penthouse, protected from the air, and quite concealed from the eye. " From this," says Linnæus, " we may see that the structure of leaves is not fortuitous, but destined by an omniscient Creator to answer some particular end."

Several causes for the difference of the state of plants during the night and during the day, have been proposed, such as the influence of light, change of temperature, and the atmospherical humidity, or these causes combined. Linnæus seems to have shewn that it is the absence of light, and not of heat, which produces the *sleep of plants,* as it has been termed; but there is still ample room for the investigation of this subject.

CHAPTER VI.

CONCLUDING REMARKS.

" Somne quies rerum, placidissime somne deorum,
Pax animi quam cura fugit ; qui corpora duris
Festa ministeriis, mulces, reparasque labore."
                                        LUCRETIUS.

WE shall now proceed in conclusion to make
a few remarks on the general management of
sleep. With regard to the quantity of sleep
requisite for health and the restoration of the
exhausted energies, so much depends upon the
constitution, age, health, habits, and employments
of the individual, that we cannot give any fixed
rule which would apply to all cases. Children
and the aged require more sleep than adults,
and women usually have need of more than

males. Generally speaking, however, from six
to eight hours will be found sufficient for most
individuals in good health. Infants during the
first month of their existence sleep almost continually, and indeed their so doing is a healthy
sign, and ought to be encouraged, as at that
early age they cannot sleep too much.

The influence of habit on the natural duration
of sleep is very remarkable.—General Elliot
never slept more than four hours out of the
twenty-four, and Gooch gives an instance of a
man who slept only for fifteen minutes out of
the twenty-four hours, and, notwithstanding
which, enjoyed good health and reached his
seventy-third year. Persons labouring under
any very great excitement, have been sometimes
known to remain for a long period without sleep :
—thus, a murderer mentioned by Schubert,
remained fourteen days and nights awake,
although he had taken from time to time, during
that period, forty grains of opium to induce

sleep.* Insane persons are known to sleep very little, and some indeed, have been said never to sleep at all. The poison of a mad dog induces amongst other symptoms continued waking. Hysterical persons also, remain sometimes for an astonishing time without sleep. Others, again, acquire a habit of sleeping very long. It is said of Quin the actor, that he could sleep twenty-four hours successively. Nothing is more injurious however, than excess of sleep. It renders the body feeble and languid, and the mind dull, melancholy and stupid, and indisposed for continued attention to any subject;—it also retards the circulation, diminishes the secretions and excretions, and engenders obesity, and incapacity for the functions of life.

Boerhaave relates the case of a young physician, who took such an inordinate love for sleep, that he retired to a quiet and obscure

* " Geschichte der Seele"

place, and slept almost continually. This per-
nicious habit, however, soon affected his understanding, and he fell into a state resembling
idiotcy. " Those who give way to slothfulness,"
says Dr. Hodgkin,* " may be said to waste life
in a threefold manner. First, all the time con-
sumed in rest and sleep, beyond what the body
and mind require, is lost; a second portion is
lost in the diminished value of their waking
hours; and thirdly, the term of their life is
likely to be shortened by the injury which their
health sustains."

Want of proper sleep, on the other hand, is
equally injurious, both to the mind and body.
Deprived of the necessary portion of sleep, a
person's mind soon becomes incapacitated for
useful exertions; the functions of the nervous
system become disordered, the memory im-
paired, he becomes listless and emaciated, and

* Lectures on the means of promoting and preserving
health. Page 293.

if the deprivation of sleep be carried to a great extent, it occasions in the end insensibility, loss of power of voluntary motion, and then vertigo, delirium, and madness. In giving want of sleep as an ordinary cause of melancholy, Burton thus describes its effects, "It causeth driness of the brain, frensie, dotage, and makes the body dry, lean, hard, and ugly to behold. The temperature of the brain is corrupted by it, the humours adust, the eyes made to sink into the head, choler increased, and the whole body inflamed; and, (as may be added out of Galen) it overthrows the natural heat; it causeth crudities, hurts concoction; and what not?*

In many diseases, want of sleep is a very obstinate symptom, and by it other existing bad symptoms are aggravated. Certain stimulating agents, such as strong tea, (especially green) coffee, &c. taken before going to bed, frequently

* Anatomy of Melancholy.

prevent the access of sleep. Any irritation of
the nervous system, or disturbed state of the
great secreting organs, almost always either
prevents sleep, or renders it imperfect. Also,
uneasy bodily feelings, great grief, cold (when
not extreme) strong mental emotions of every
kind, and long continued application to study
all tend to cause sleeplessness.

" Cold and heat constitute the most simple,
and often the most efficacious means of inducing
sleep, or of tranquillising it, or of relieving it
from its torpor. Sponging the whole surface of
the skin with cold, or tepid, or hot water;
fomenting the feet and legs with warm water;
the application of cold or warm water to the
head; these often constitute sufficiently energetic
and perfectly safe sedatives, and are often the
simple but effectual means of procuring for the
invalid the restorative blessing of perfect sleep.

"To secure sleep, that most necessary appen-
dage to health and happiness, the mind must be

tranquil, its powers moderately used, but not
over worked, and its several faculties kept in
proper subjection to one another; the muscles
of voluntary motion must be exercised; the
stomach kept free from disturbance; the circu-
lating and respiratory organs, the functions of
secretion and excretion, all perform their several
duties without appreciable inconvenience; and,
to promote the same end, the bed room should
be well ventilated and cool, the bed somewhat
hard, the bed clothes sufficient to maintain the
bodily heat, without unduly confining it, the
room should be dark, and the silence perfect."*

Drowsiness, or a frequent disposition to sleep,
is a common attendant on old age, and we often
find old or elderly people dosing in their chairs,
or when attempting to read, and sometimes even
during their meals. Drowsiness may also proceed from a disordered state of the digestive

* Robertson on Diet and Regimen.—3rd Edition.
p. 247.

organs, or from fulness of blood in the head, and is sometimes a symptom of apoplexy and other diseases, in which cases, it will disappear with the exciting causes. A tendency to frequent sleep may be often conquered by various means; sometimes a strong resolution to keep awake is sufficient, or engaging in mental or bodily exercise, or in fact by whatever is capable of vividly exciting the senses. If we have passed our usual time for yielding to sleep, the inclination to do so sometimes passes off for some hours.

There can be no doubt that early rising is one of the best conducives to health, and we will find that many of the most distinguished men in all times have been early risers. Alfred the Great, Sir Thomas More, Paley, Buffon, Franklin, Priestley, Napoleon, Frederick the Great, and Charles the XIIth, are reported to have been early risers, and amongst the most celebrated of our countrymen at the present day, we may mention as early risers, the Duke of Wellington and

Lord Brougham. Sir John Sinclair, in his
" Code of health and longevity," has stated, that
all of a great number of very old persons, whom he
questioned, *were alike in two particulars,*—they
were descended from parents of good constitution,
and, (what perhaps they would better affirm)—
they were early risers. Indeed, we have only to
look at the health and cheerfulness depicted upon
the countenances of our farmers and peasantry
in evidence of this salutary habit. Many persons
find a difficulty in commencing the practice of
early rising, not knowing how to get into the
habit by degrees ; and will rise two or three
mornings at five, and then relapse into their former late hours. John Wesley, in his " Treatise
on early rising," gives the following excellent
method of ascertaining how much sleep a person
really requires. " If any one desire to know
exactly what quantity of sleep his own constitution requires, he may very easily make the experiment which I made about sixty years ago :

I then waked every night about twelve or one, and lay awake for some time. I readily concluded that this arose from my lying longer in bed than nature required. To be satisfied, I procured an alarum which awaked me the next morning at seven (near an hour earlier than I arose the day before), yet I lay awake again at night. The second morning I arose at six ; but notwithstanding this, I lay awake the second night. The third morning I arose at five ; but nevertheless, I lay awake the third night. The fourth morning I arose at four (as by the grace of God I have done ever since), and I lay awake no more. And I do not now lie awake, (taking the year round) a quarter of an hour together in a month. By the same experiment, rising earlier and earlier every morning, may any one find how much sleep he really wants."

Nothing tends more to the continuance of good health, to repair the wasted energies of the body, and to the prolongation of life, than *undisturbed* sleep, enjoyed at regular periods and in moderation.

"Verum ut somnus ad prolongationem vitae facit, ita multo magis, si sit placidus et non turbidus."

BACON ;

Sleep produces good effects in most diseases, especially in inflammatory ones of the thorax, and abdomen ; and means should be taken in these cases to induce it if possible. It is particularly productive of good in diseases accompanied by pain, which it greatly mitigates. It is also beneficial after certain surgical operations, and in the treatment of fractures and dislocations. Any extraordinary variation of the phenomena occurring in natural sleep should be attentively remarked by the physician, and it is of importance, in examinations of this nature, to take into consideration the usual habits of the individual; as some persons naturally present, during sleep, certain singularities, which in others would be regarded as dangerous symptoms. Sleep troubled with terrible dreams, frequent startings, and convulsive motions, generally indicates great irritability of the brain or its membrane, and is a dangerous symptom. Should the sleep of an invalid which has been for some time past disturbed, again become tranquil and natural, it may be regarded as a favourable symptom. It is important in diseases to distinguish that sleep which is healthy and augurs favourably from one which is unrefreshing and hurtful, adding to the severity of the symptoms. The first is tranquil, equable and light, is known by its salutary effects, and is almost always the presage of a favourable termination : the second is agitated, heavy, and unrefreshing, and diminishes instead of adds to the strength.

Since, therefore, sleep is a condition so essential to our health, happiness, and pro-

131

longation of life, it is obvious of what importance it is to attend to a proper and due
regulation of it, so as to allow the energies of
nature to be recruited, and health and vigour
to be imparted both to the mind and body.
Since also, sleep is such an invaluable auxiliary
in the treatment of disease, it becomes the duty
of every physician to be fully acquainted with
the phenomena presented by it in health and
sickness.—" Ad vitam et sanitatem conser-
vandas, somnus non utilis modo, sed prorsus
necessarius; et ad multos morbos, sanandos
vel levandos præstantissimum remedium.*

* Gregory.

FINIS.

EDMUND FRY AND SON, Printers, Bishopsgate Street.

For EU product safety concerns, contact us at Calle de José Abascal, 56–1°,
28003 Madrid, Spain or eugpsr@cambridge.org.

 www.ingramcontent.com/pod-product-compliance
Ingram Content Group UK Ltd.
Pitfield, Milton Keynes, MK11 3LW, UK
UKHW012339130625
459647UK00009B/389